Howard Kasschau

PIANO COURSE

Step-by-Step to Mastery of the Piano

PRIVATE or CLASS INSTRUCTION

Illustrated by Josine Ianco Kline

ED. 2347

G. SCHIRMER, Inc.

DISTRIBUTED BY

HAL•LEONARD®
CORPORATION
7777 W. BLUEMOUND RD. P.O. BOX 13819 MILWAUKEE, WI 53213

CONTENTS

TO THE TEACHER

This book serves a two-fold purpose: (1) It is a continuation of *TEACH ME TO PLAY* and may be introduced during the latter part of the first year's instruction. (2) It may be used as a first book for the older beginner, covering approximately a year's work.

The material in this book ranges from a presentation of practice procedures through the establishment of the hand positions for the keys of *C G* and *F,* to compositions that fully explore these keys.

The student will become familiar with the damper pedal, being carefully instructed in its use. Original material is supplied that accentuates correct pedalling in practice and performance.

The student is introduced to the use of the metronome, and pieces employing various tempi are included.

Harmonic awareness is developed through the explanation of intervals, and both major and minor triads.

Book I concludes with a presentation of the scales and arpeggios in their simplest forms.

Howard Kasschau

4

LEARNING TO READ MUSIC

Piano music is written upon two staffs. At the beginning of each staff is a clef sign:

The G Clef

The F Clef

Middle C appears
in two positions:

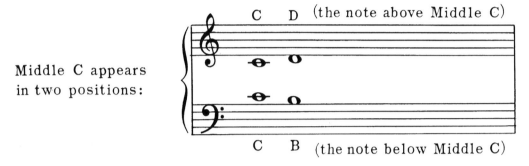

Memorize the location upon the keyboard of the following notes by reciting the words and playing the keys:

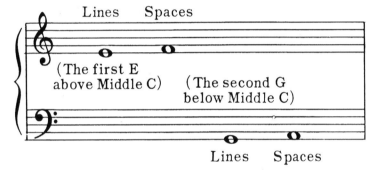

Memorize the following groups of lines and spaces:

1. Every Good Boy Does Fine.
2. F A C E.
3. Great Big Dreams For America.
4. All Cows Eat Grass.

Recite and play the following groups of lines and spaces:

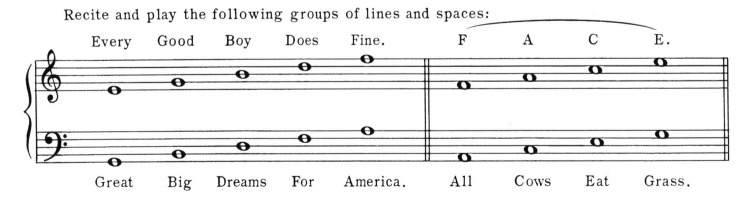

To the Teacher

The following notes are unrelated. They provide an exercise in note-reading and are to be continued until complete security is attained. The notes may be played in numerical order *or* they may be called at random by the teacher, parent or older student.

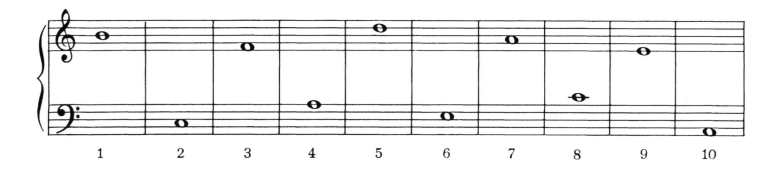

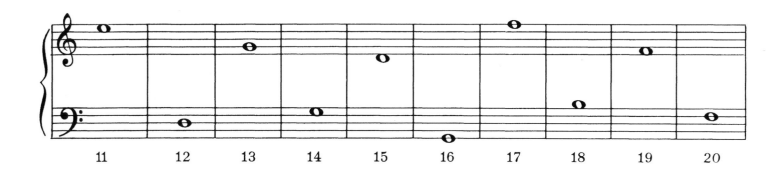

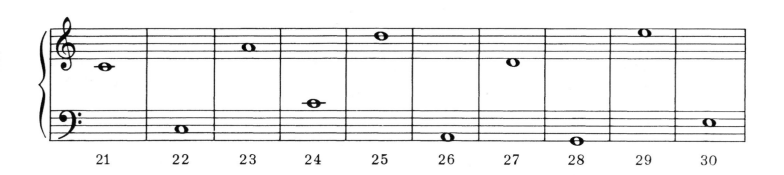

LEARNING HOW TO PRACTICE

When learning a new piece of music it is necessary to notice the following things:

1. The Key Signature:

A key signature is a group of sharps or flats just after the clef signs. If there is no key signature the piece is written in the Key of C.

2. The Time Signature:

The *upper* number tells you how many counts are in each measure. The *lower* number tells you what kind of note receives one count.

3. The note and rest values that are being used:

NOTE	REST	NAME	VALUE
♩	𝄽	Quarter-	1 Count
♩	▬	Half-	2 Counts
♩.		Dotted half-	3 Counts
𝅝	▬	Whole	4 Counts

4. The position of the hands upon the keyboard.

The most satisfactory results are obtained by learning *one phrase* at a time. A PHRASE is a group of measures that express a musical thought, as words do in speaking and writing. The hands are now placed in the following position:

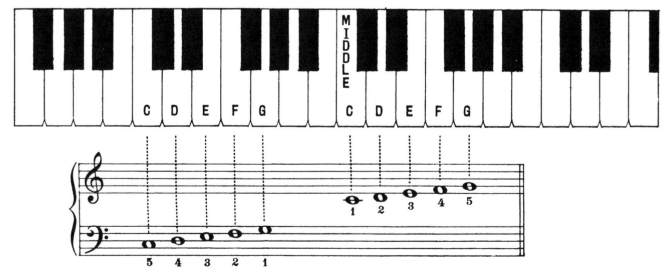

This is called THE C POSITION.

The right hand alone plays the first phrase:

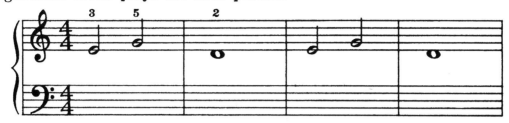

Then the left hand alone plays the first phrase:

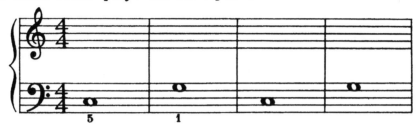

This is called PRACTICING HANDS SEPARATELY.

We are now ready to play the first phrase by PLAYING HANDS TOGETHER.

Any new piece is more easily learned this way – phrase by phrase, first playing the phrase *hands separately* and then playing the phrase *hands together*. Apply this WORK METHOD to your first piece.

Play A Tune

LEGATO

The basic touch used at the keyboard is called *legato*. It means smooth, even, connected. **To pro-**duce a perfect *legato* it is necessary to transfer the *relaxed* arm weight from one finger tip to another, lifting each finger at the precise instant the next finger plays.

If the following preparatory study is carefully worked out, it will produce a **perfect** *legato*.

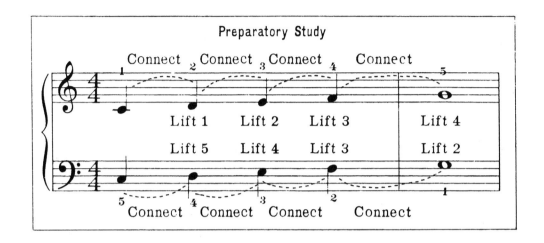

On the River

The Phrase Line

A curved line (⌣ or ⌣), called a PHRASE LINE (or SLUR), is used to show those notes that are to be played in one group. All notes under the phrase line are to be played *legato*. At the end of each phrase line the hands are *released* from the keyboard by using the phrasing touch.

THE PHRASING TOUCH

Think of the words DOWN-UP, DOWN-UP. Then place the finger tips on the keys and slowly raise and lower the wrist several times. When the wrists are completely loose, then lift the hands, wrist first, from the keyboard. This is the PHRASING TOUCH.

Down a Country Lane

RHYTHM
$\frac{4}{4}$ RHYTHM

RHYTHM is a regular grouping of heavy counts and light counts within a measure. In all rhythms the accent is on the first count. An accent occurs when more stress or pressure is applied to one tone than is applied to the others. The *Theme* from the *Ninth Symphony* is in 4/4 rhythm.

Preparatory Study	
Count: ONE two three four	ONE two three four
Recite: HEAVY light light light	HEAVY light light light

Theme
from the *Ninth Symphony*

Ludwig van Beethoven

Ludwig van Beethoven is one of the greatest names in musical history. He started the study of music at the age of four. During his lifetime as a composer, he developed the symphony and the sonata to their highest forms.

His work habits were very strict. He carried sketchbooks with him at all times and wrote down musical ideas as they occurred to him. Then would begin a tireless reworking of those ideas until they finally pleased him.

(1770-1827)

$\frac{3}{4}$ RHYTHM

Dutch Dance is written in $\frac{3}{4}$ rhythm. The accent is again on the first count, but is followed by two light counts.

Preparatory Study	
Count: ONE two three	ONE two three
Recite: HEAVY light light	HEAVY light light

Dutch Dance

This is a WALTZ rhythm, as you hear in well-known waltzes like *The Blue Danube* by Johann Strauss.

THE TIE

A CURVED LINE ‿

connecting **two notes on the** *same* line or space is called a TIE. The second note is held for its *full* value without being sounded again.

Play   Hold

The Butterfly Queen

$\frac{2}{4}$ RHYTHM

Teeter-Totter is in $\frac{2}{4}$ rhythm. The accent is on the first count and there is one light count following it in each measure.

Preparatory Study	
Count: ONE two	ONE two
Recite: HEAVY light	HEAVY light

Teeter-Totter

When the five fingers of each hand are over five adjacent keys, the hand is in the *five-finger position.* Fingering patterns are based on this fundamental position. It is sometimes necessary to put a finger *over* the thumb or the thumb *under* a finger in order to move from one position to another.

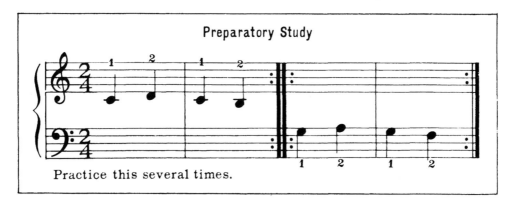

Hop-o'-my-thumb

Usually the right hand plays in the Treble clef and the left hand plays in the Bass clef. But special effects are created when both hands play in the same clef. When the left hand notes are written in the Treble clef, the lines and spaces are read in the same manner as they would be if the right hand were playing them. When the right hand notes are written in the Bass Clef, the lines and spaces are read in the same manner as they would be if the left hand were playing them.

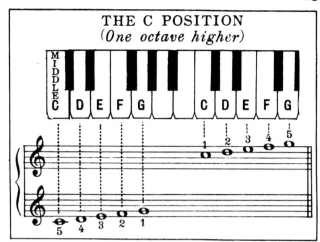

THE C POSITION
(One octave higher)

A Song of Spring

German Folk Song

Sing, sing, sing! For to - day is Spring.
(Both hands in the G Clef)

Flow-ers bloom-ing, plants are grow-ing, Trees are green, their leaves are show-ing;

Sing, sing, sing! For to - day is Spring.
(Both hands in the F Clef)

*THE C POSITION
(One octave lower)

"Rolling River" from the collection *Five Easy Pieces* by Howard Kasschau, published by G. Schirmer, Inc., may be presented at this time. It is a black-key study, with crossing hands, in the key of F♯, and in 4/4 time. It is an interesting recital piece.

THE SCALE OF C MAJOR

Up to now all of the pieces have been played upon the white keys. No black keys (called sharps or flats) have been used. We have been playing in the key of C MAJOR. The tones that make up the KEY of C MAJOR can be arranged in such an order that they form a SCALE.

This is the SCALE of C MAJOR:

The SCALE of C MAJOR begins and ends on C.

When some tones of a scale are played separately they form a MELODY:

When some tones of a scale are played together they form a CHORD:

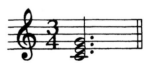

THREE-IN-ONE

THE SCALE OF C MAJOR *(continued)*

The SCALE of C MAJOR, like every other scale, is made up of a combination of WHOLE STEPS and HALF-STEPS.

A HALF-STEP is the distance between any two keys which have NO KEY IN BETWEEN.

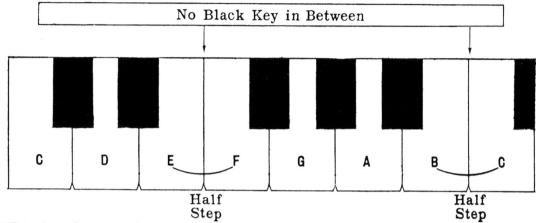

A WHOLE STEP is the distance between any two keys which have ONE KEY IN BETWEEN.

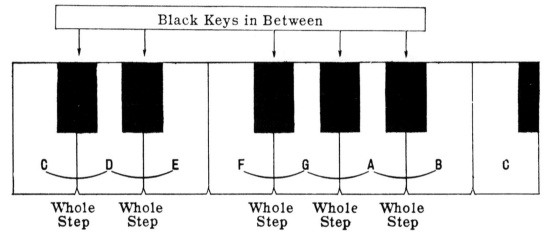

The following diagram shows you the order of WHOLE STEPS and HALF-STEPS used to form the SCALE OF C MAJOR.

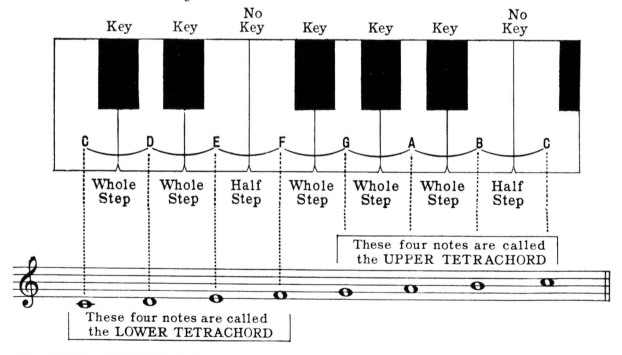

The UPPER TETRACHORD of one scale becomes the LOWER TETRACHORD of the *next* scale. For instance, the upper tetrachord of the scale of C major becomes the lower tetrachord of the key of G major, etc.

CHORD BUILDING
Intervals

An *interval* is the *difference* in pitch between two tones. It is known by the number of lines and spaces it includes.

From C to D is a SECOND. It is two tones from the lower tone to the upper tone.

From C to E is a THIRD. It is three tones from the lower tone to the upper tone.

From C to F is a FOURTH. It is four tones from the lower tone to the upper tone.

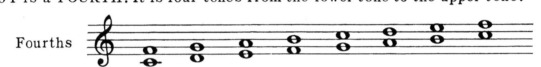

From C to G is a FIFTH. It is five tones from the lower tone to the upper tone.

From C to A is a SIXTH. It is six tones from the lower tone to the upper tone.

From C to B is a SEVENTH. It is seven tones from the lower tone to the upper tone.

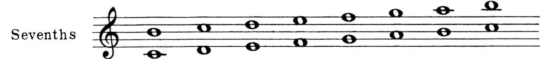

From C to C is an OCTAVE. It is eight tones from the lower tone to the upper tone.

THE TRIAD

A three-toned chord is called a TRIAD. It consists of:

a ROOT:    a THIRD above the root: a FIFTH above the root:

A triad (consisting of a root, third and fifth) may be built on *any* tone of a scale. The letter name of the root determines the name of the triad:

C triad (Major)   D triad (minor)   E triad (minor)   F triad (Major)   G triad (Major)   A triad (minor)   B triad (diminished)

Because the root tones of the above triads are at the bottom, the triads are in ROOT POSITION.

Triad Inversions

When the THIRD of the triad is at the bottom, the triad is in the FIRST INVERSION:

When the FIFTH of the triad is at the bottom, the triad is in the SECOND INVERSION:

All triads may appear in three positions:

The C Major Triad

Root Position   First Inversion   Second Inversion
(the *third* at the bottom) (the *fifth* at the bottom)

The F Major Triad

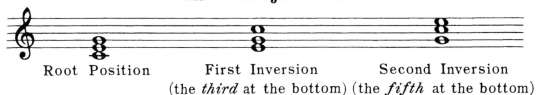

Root Position   First Inversion   Second Inversion
(the *third* at the bottom) (the *fifth* at the bottom)

The G Major Triad

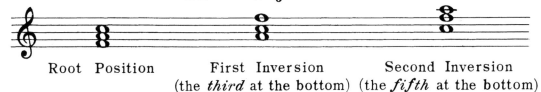

Root Position   First Inversion   Second Inversion
(the *third* at the bottom) (the *fifth* at the bottom)

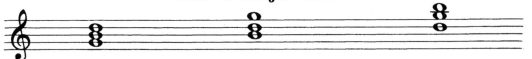

THE SCALE OF G MAJOR

A sharp(♯) placed before a note *raises* a tone a half-step.

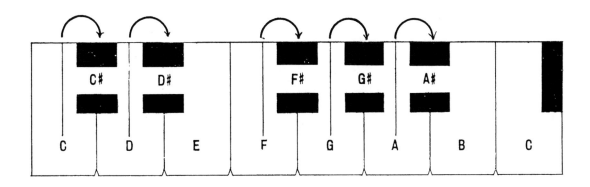

THE SCALE of G MAJOR begins and ends on G. It is made up of the same combination of whole steps and half-steps as the Scale of C Major. The next to the last note is F♯.

Tug-of-War

Some teachers may want to introduce the *sharp scales* in their simplest form at this point. They will be found, together with a simple arpeggio and the key chord, on page 61.

THE KEY OF G MAJOR

This is a key signature:

The sharp after each clef sign (*the key signature*) tells you that every F in the piece is to be played F-SHARP. Since the piece begins and ends on G and every F is sharped, we are playing in the KEY OF G MAJOR.

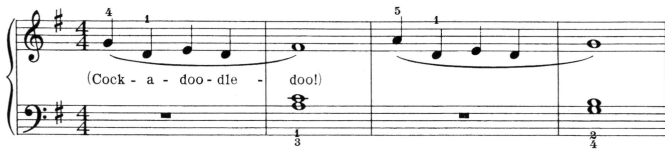

Cock-a-doodle-doo

(Cock - a - doo - dle - doo!)

THE G POSITION

Sailboat on the Lake

THE ARPEGGIO

When the tones of a chord are played separately they form a broken chord.

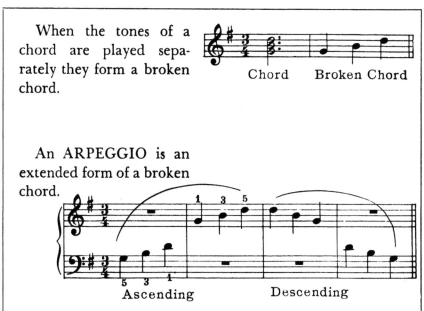

Chord   Broken Chord

An ARPEGGIO is an extended form of a broken chord.

Ascending   Descending

The Ferris Wheel

The Ferris wheel stops and we're at the top.

Now we are down and back on the ground.

A single EIGHTH-NOTE looks like this: ♪

Two EIGHTH-NOTES look like this: ♫

An EIGHTH-REST looks like this: ⅄

EIGHTH-NOTES are FAST NOTES. Two Eighth-notes are played in one count.

Tapping Exercise

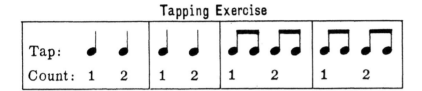

Follow the Leader

BENDING WILLOW TREES is a study in chord play-ing. All tones in chords must be played *precisely together*. This requires the simultaneous playing of both hands *and* the simultaneous playing of the fingers within each hand.

Place the hands in position for the first chord and play it several times until all tones sound exactly together.

Bending Willow Trees

"Japan Garden" from the collection *Five Easy Pieces* by Howard Kasschau, a study in repose and quiet mood-building, may be introduced at this time.

Folk melodies are stories in song of everyday events. Until recently folk songs were handed down from one generation to another without being written on paper.

Most folk songs are of unknown origin. However, this tune was actually composed by Jean Baptiste Lully (1632-1687), who was the court composer of Louis XIV, King of France.

Au Clair de la Lune was so attractive that it quickly achieved the popularity of a folk song. Be sure to phrase this piece properly.

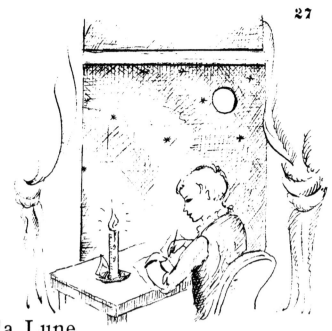

Au Clair de la Lune
(In the Pale Moonlight)

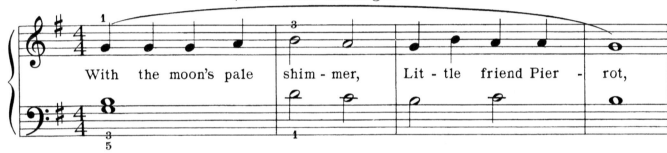

With the moon's pale shim - mer, Lit - tle friend Pier - rot,

Shines thy can - dle's glim - mer On the fal - len snow.

Lend a pen, I pray thee, But a word to write,

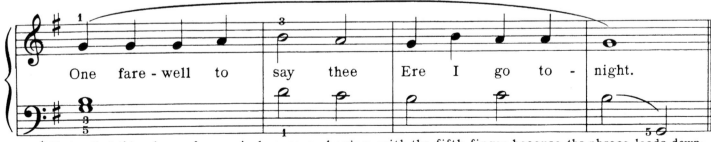

One fare - well to say thee Ere I go to - night.

* Notice that this phrase, for musical reasons, begins with the fifth finger because the phrase leads downward to D

The short three-note runs (two eighth-notes and a quarter-note) which appear throughout *LAZY LUKE* are preparatory studies for the development of speed. Be careful to play the three-note groups in a connected manner, the eighth-notes going *to* the quarter-note without hesitation. This will create a feeling of motion which is an element of all music.

Lazy Luke

CROSS-HAND PLAYING

When one hand leaves its usual clef and crosses the other hand, it is called the *Visiting Hand*. A simple rule to remember is that the *Visiting Hand* always goes OVER the other hand.

Burning Logs

(This is the second C above middle C)

THE SCALE OF F MAJOR

A flat (♭) placed before a note *lowers* a tone a half-step.

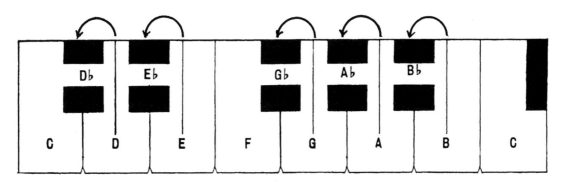

THE SCALE of F MAJOR begins and ends on F. It is made up of the same combination of whole steps and half-steps as the scales of C major and G major. The fourth note is B♭.

Falling Snow

(Scale of F Major)

Some teachers may want to introduce the *flat scales* in their simplest form at this point. They will be found, together with a simple arpeggio and the key chord, on page 62.

THE KEY OF F MAJOR

The key signature for this piece is one flat:

The flats after the clef signs *(the key signature)* tell you that every B in the piece is to be played B-FLAT. Since the piece begins and ends on F, and every B is flatted, we are playing in the KEY OF F MAJOR.

The Apple Orchard

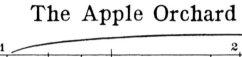

THE F POSITION

Gull on the Wave

A DOT over or under a note ( ) makes it short. This touch is called STACCATO. We now have two different touches at the keyboard:

LEGATO — smooth, even, connected
STACCATO — short and detached

THE STACCATO TOUCH

THE STACCATO TOUCH is easily learned in the following manner:

1. Place the hands upon the keys in the C Position.
2. Very quickly throw the hands into the keys and then up, wrist first, high into the air.
3. The touch is completed with the hands hanging in the air above the keyboard.

Jack in the Box

"Tick Tock" from the collection *Five Easy Pieces* by Howard Kasschau may be presented at this time. It is a study in contrasting legato and staccato touches. The left hand occasionally plays the melody.

EXPRESSION SIGNS

To make our playing more interesting we use EXPRESSION SIGNS. We do this by *changing* the loudness and softness of the tones in our pieces. Here is a table of the most often used EXPRESSION SIGNS and their meanings:

p (piano)	Soft
mp (mezzo-piano)	Medium soft
f (forte)	Loud
mf (mezzo-forte)	Medium loud
< *(crescendo)*	To grow louder
> *(diminuendo)*	To grow softer
Ritardando (Ritard. or Rit.) . .	To slow down

You can make your playing much more interesting if you follow these signs.

Down in the Valley

American Folk Song

ver, Hear the wind blow,

Hear the wind blow, dear, Hear the wind

blow, Hang your head o -

ritard.

ver, Hear the wind blow.

As the frontiers expanded in the early days of America, the men and women at the end of a day's work spent many evenings in singing games. Dancing, singing, fiddle-playing and hand-clapping provided them with relaxation.

Skip To My Lou is the story of a bashful boy, surrounded by singing couples; he shyly chooses a partner only to have her stolen by another.

Play *Skip To My Lou* rather fast and with a strong rhythm to portray the energy and happy mood of the dance.

Skip To My Lou

American Folk Song

This is one of the most popular American folk songs. It is a reminder of the time when sleeping in a goose-feather bed was a luxury.

All barnyard creatures have been given personality in songs. *Go Tell Aunt Nancy* is a song about a goose. Its verses tell how Aunt Nancy lost her feather-bed when her best goose was drowned in a millpond.

Go Tell Aunt Nancy

American Folk Song

Long, Long Ago is a romantic love song that has been popular for many generations. It is sung by both children and adults. Very little is known of the composer, Bayly, although many of his songs have been used by folk singers.

Play *Long, Long Ago* quietly and slowly to emphasize the sadness of the song. A slight *crescendo* as the melody rises and a slight *diminuendo* as it descends will increase the beauty of this piece.

Long, Long Ago

Thomas H. Bayly

DOTTED NOTE VALUES

A note followed by a dot is lengthened by half of its own value:

Tapping Exercise

Tap:	♩.	♪	♩.	♪	♩.	♪	♩.	♪
Count:	1	2	1	2	1	2	1	2

Largo
from the *New World Symphony*

Antonin Dvořák

Dvořák was a famous Bohemian composer, the son of an innkeeper. His musical gifts were evident from his earliest years. When he was only eight years old he played in his father's band.

In 1892, after he had become world-famous, he came to America where he lived and worked for three years. Here he wrote the well-known symphony which he called *From the New World*.

(1841-1904)

SINGING MELODY AND ACCOMPANIMENT

In this German folk song, the right hand plays the melody and the left hand plays the accompaniment. The melody (right hand) should be played *louder* than the accompaniment (left hand) because musically it is more important. The difference in loudness between the melody and accompaniment is called BALANCE.

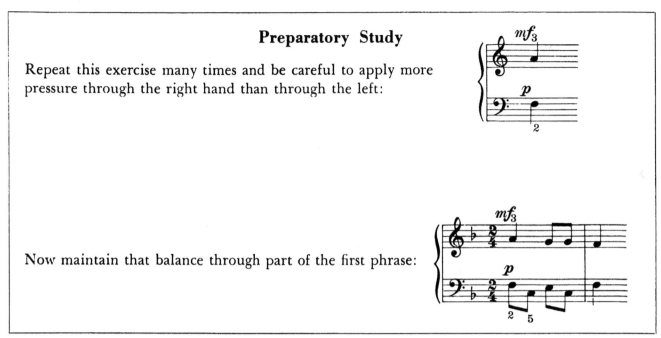

Preparatory Study

Repeat this exercise many times and be careful to apply more pressure through the right hand than through the left:

Now maintain that balance through part of the first phrase:

Sleep, Baby, Sleep

German Folk Song

THE NATURAL SIGN

A NATURAL SIGN (♮) is used to change a sharped or flatted tone *back* to its natural key. Any sign (sharp, flat or natural) that is not in the key signature but is next to a note is called an ACCIDENTAL. An accidental remains in effect *only* during the measure in which it appears. The next bar line restores the sharps or flats that are in the key signature.

The Sleeping Rose

* Notice that this phrase, for musical reasons, begins with the fourth finger because the phrase ends on low D.

THE PEDALS

Large, modern pianos have three pedals: the *Damper* or *Loud Pedal* (at the right), the *Tone Sustaining Pedal* (in the center), and the *Soft Pedal* (at the left). Smaller pianos, such as spinets, do not always have a middle pedal.

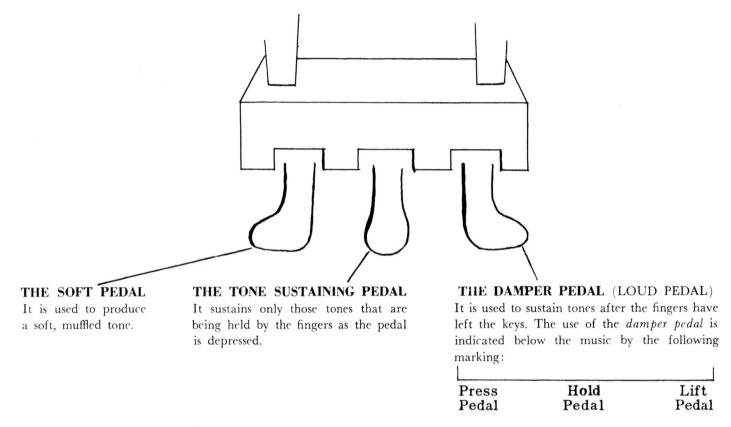

THE SOFT PEDAL
It is used to produce a soft, muffled tone.

THE TONE SUSTAINING PEDAL
It sustains only those tones that are being held by the fingers as the pedal is depressed.

THE DAMPER PEDAL (LOUD PEDAL)
It is used to sustain tones after the fingers have left the keys. The use of the *damper pedal* is indicated below the music by the following marking:

| Press | Hold | Lift |
| Pedal | Pedal | Pedal |

For a thorough study of the use of the pedals, *The First Grade Pedal Book* by Howard Kasschau may be introduced at this point.

The Harp in the Trees

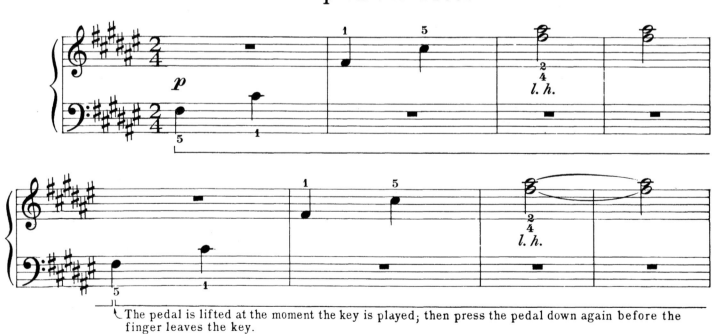

⌐ The pedal is lifted at the moment the key is played; then press the pedal down again before the finger leaves the key.

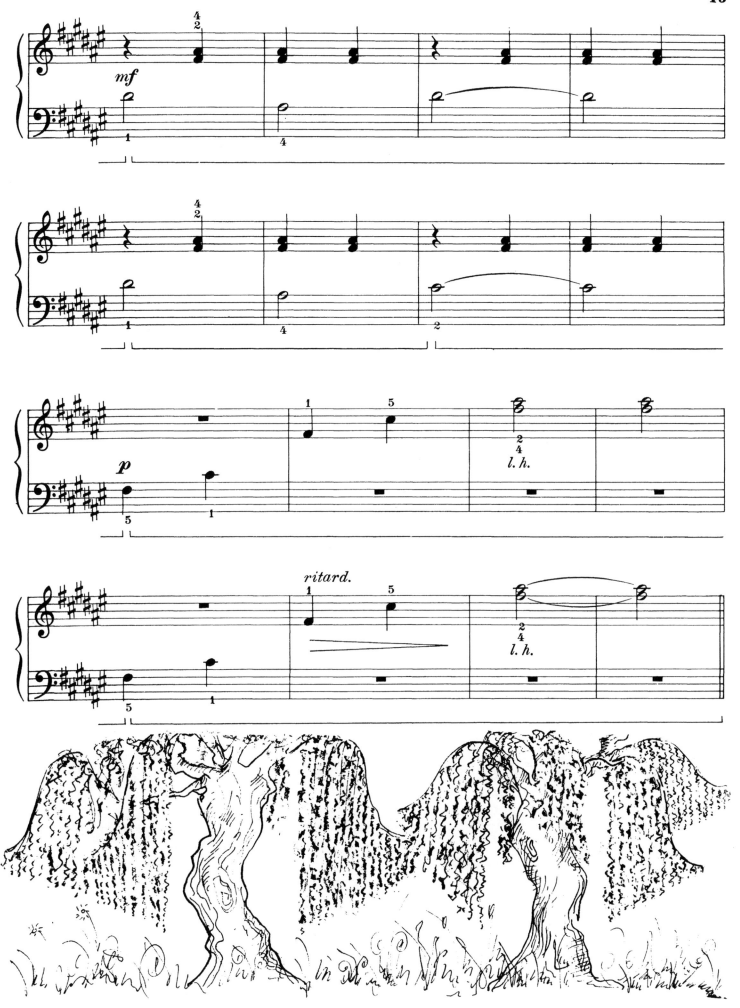

Mozart is one of the world's greatest composers. His talent for music was so great that at the age of five he was composing minuets; at six he was composing concertos; at eleven a Mass and, at nineteen, his first opera. He made many concert tours in Europe with his sister, Nannerl. Throughout his life he was a successful and popular performer. The melody of *Twinkle, Twinkle Little Star* has been attributed to Mozart who used it for a set of attractive variations. It has been used by many other composers as well and is sometimes called the *Alphabet Song*.

(1756-1791)

Twinkle, Twinkle Little Star

Wolfgang Amadeus Mozart

"Giant Steps" from the collection *Five Easy Pieces* by Howard Kasschau is a study in fifths, and affords an interesting recital piece at this point.

THE UP-BEAT

Music does not always begin with the first count of the measure. Sometimes it begins on a *light beat* which is *before the bar line* and is called the UP-BEAT. However, the accent must be on the first note *after* the bar line.

Tapping Exercise

Count: Three	ONE two three	ONE two
Recite: Light	HEAVY light light	HEAVY light

The count before the bar line at the very beginning of the piece and the counts in the last measure of the piece equal one full measure.

Good Morning

American Singing Game

THE MINOR KEYS
(The Parallel Minor Approach)

So far, all of the pieces have been written in what are called MAJOR KEYS. Major Keys express joyful moods. For contrast, there are also keys that express serious moods. These are called MINOR KEYS.

There is a Minor Key, or Scale, that is related to each Major Key, or Scale. A Minor Scale is easily formed by lowering the third and sixth steps of the Major Scale by a half-step.

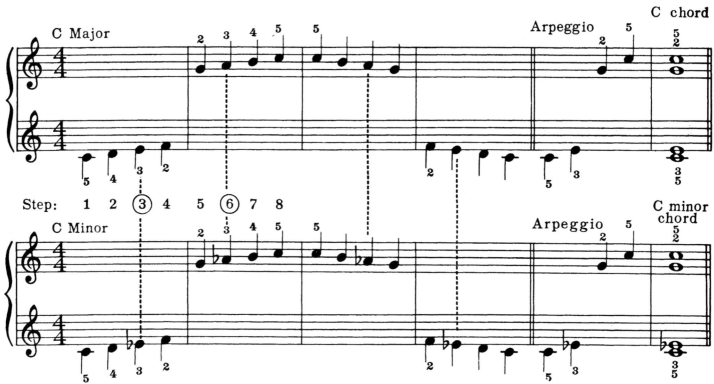

Both the scale of C Major and the scale of C Minor begin on C and use the same letter names. The C Minor scale is called the PARALLEL MINOR to C Major. You may change each one of the Major Scales on pages 61 and 62 to its Parallel Minor by lowering the third and sixth steps by a half-step (in other words, the third finger of each hand.)

MAJOR AND MINOR TRIADS

A *major triad* may be changed to a *minor triad* by *lowering* the third of the major triad a half-step:

A *minor triad* may be changed to a *major triad* by *raising* the third of the minor triad a half-step:

Go Down, Moses

Go Down, Moses is written in the key of A minor, the parallel key to the key of A major.

⁶⁄₈ RHYTHM

This is a new time signature:

There are six counts in a measure.
An eighth-note receives one count.

We now have a new set of time values:

♪ = 1 Count

♩ = 2 Counts

♩. = 3 Counts

𝅗𝅥. = 6 Counts

The accents are on the first and fourth counts, each accent being followed by two light counts.

Tapping Exercise

Count: ONE two three FOUR five six	ONE two three FOUR five six
Recite: HEAVY light light HEAVY light light	HEAVY light light HEAVY light light

The Bagpipe Bagatelle

Little Avalanche is a preparatory study for "L'Avalanche" by Stephen Heller (opus 47). It is a velocity (speed) study and should be played rapidly and brilliantly.

It is also a study in contrasting touches. The eighth-note triplets are to be played *legato*. Lift the fingers *high* to produce a brilliant tone. The chords are to be played with a *forearm staccato*. This touch is produced by using the hand, wrist and forearm as a single unit which is moved from the elbow.

Little Avalanche

TRIPLETS

A TRIPLET (♪♪♪) occurs when three eighth-notes are played in one count. Here is a tapping exercise:

The number *3* appears in italics over the triplet. This is not to be confused with any numbers that might be used during the triplet to indicate fingering.

Whirlwind

TEMPO MARKINGS

At the beginning of most pieces you will find a word (or a group of words) to indicate both the speed and character of the music. These indications are called *Tempo Markings*. They are usually written in Italian, which is the accepted international language of music.

Tempo means *rate of speed*. The tempo markings most commonly used are:

Largo — very slow, broad

Adagio — slow, at ease

Lento — slow, not dragging

Andante — fairly slow, easily flowing

Moderato — moderately moving

Allegretto — moderately fast

Allegro — fast, lively

Presto — very fast

The Metronome

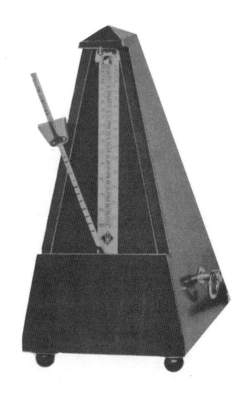

Sometimes, at the beginning of a piece, you will see a note followed by a number. It looks like this $\quart$ = 96. This is called a *metronome marking,* and it tells you exactly how fast or how slow to play the piece. For instance, if you see at the beginning of a composition the marking $\quart$ = 96 you set your metronome at the number marked 96. Then you listen briefly to the sound of the metronome and then play the piece at the resulting speed. Every quarter note ($\quart$) is played to equal the sound of one tick of the metronome.

Some compositions are written primarily for dancing. Naturally, such a piece will have a strong and definite rhythm so that the dance steps may be even and graceful.

A waltz is a dance in three-four rhythm and is one of the most graceful and popular of all dance forms. Waltzes vary from slow to moderately fast tempos.

You Fill My Heart is a well-known melody in waltz rhythm. A steady, even tempo is required at all times and the expression is supplied by following the loud and soft indications.

You Fill My Heart

Allegretto

German Folk Song

You, you, you fill my heart, dear.

You, you, you please my eye.

54

Alternating-Hand Playing

When a melody is divided between two hands it is often necessary for the hands to cross over each other several times. Each arpeggio in *Pathway to the Moon* is played with alternating hands. The first note in each measure is played with the left hand and the second and third notes are played with the right hand.

The left hand should move from one position to another with a graceful, loose motion of the wrist. *Lower* the wrist as the key is played and *raise* the wrist as the finger leaves the key. The right hand must move in a quiet, sideways motion to prevent getting in the way of the left hand.

Pathway to the Moon

THE TWO-NOTE PHRASE

The phrasing touch (*down-up*) often appears in two-note groups. Its purpose is to impart grace and musicality to performance. The phrasing touch is indicated by a slur over (or under) the two notes requiring this touch. The two-note phrasing touch is easily learned by observing the following three steps:

1. As the first tone is played, the hand and wrist are level.
2. As the second tone is approached, the wrist is slowly raised.
3. As the second tone is played, the hand is lifted from the keyboard.

Tchaikovsky, whose music is loved everywhere, was born in Votkinsk, Russia. His father was a government mining inspector and his mother a French immigrant. His great musical talent was inspired by the piano lessons he received at an early age from his governess.

Throughout his life his shy, sensitive nature attracted few close friends and those were mostly other fine musicians. His whole life, both as a boy and as a man, was devoted to music. He wrote symphonies, concertos, operas, ballets, songs and piano pieces. In 1892 he visited America to participate in the dedication concerts for Carnegie Hall in New York City.

Marche Slav was written in 1877. The melody given here is one of the several stirring national airs of Serbia that Tchaikovsky used in its composition.

(1840-1893)

Marche Slav

Peter Ilyitch Tchaikovsky

"Spooks Galore" from the collection *Seven Easy Pieces* by Howard Kasschau may be presented at this time. It is a study in staccato and strict rhythm in the key of d minor and in 4/4 time.

White keys are occasionally called sharps *or* flats. Since F is a half-step above E it is sometimes called E♯. Since C is a half-step above B it is sometimes called B♯. In a similar manner E may be called F♭ and B may be called C♭.

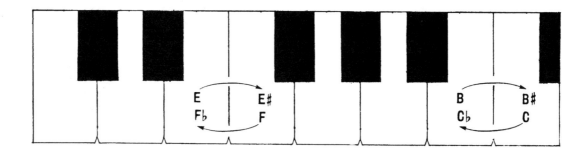

Look for the C-flats in measures 13 and 14.

Chinese Flower Market

* A grace-note (♪) is used to *embellish* a melody line. It appears as a smaller note and is played very rapidly. It is usually connected by a slur to the melody note that it embellishes.

*Notice that this phrase, for musical reasons, begins with the third finger because the phrase leads upward to Gb.

(1797-1828)

Schubert lived his entire life in Vienna, Austria. He was one of the greatest composers of melodies the world has ever known. Though he lived only thirty-one years, he composed more than six hundred songs, eight symphonies, and a great many works for all combinations of voices and instruments.

Throughout his short life he was a poor but happy man, constantly in the company of his many good friends. He composed because he *had* to, often when he had hardly enough money to buy manuscript paper. Beethoven, during his last illness, read some of Schubert's songs with delight, exclaiming that Schubert "possesses the spark of divine fire."

This theme is from his Eighth Symphony. The symphony was never completed and is known as the *Unfinished Symphony*.

Theme
from the *Unfinished Symphony*

Franz Schubert

THE SHARP MAJOR SCALES

THE FLAT MAJOR SCALES

CERTIFICATE AWARD

This Award certifies that

....

has successfully completed

BOOK ONE

and is now ready to advance to

BOOK TWO

of

THE *Howard Kasschau Piano Course*

Teacher

Date